ESSENTIAL ELEMENTS

A COMPREHENSIVE BAND METHOD

by

Tom C. Rhodes • Donald Bierschenk • Tim Lautzenheiser • John Higgins

Dear Band Student,

CONGRATULATIONS! You have graduated to the next level of your band experience and are ready to enjoy a new beginning of exciting benefits designed for you and your fellow musicians.

Have you noticed how much better you are playing, counting, listening, and enjoying band? The many hours of quality practice are opening up new opportunities for everyone in your group. You are ready to move to the next level of challenging musical benefits, and they await you in the following pages.

There are so many extra rewards band people enjoy: working together in harmony, performing for parents and friends, having a family of fellow musicians, being recognized by others as a talented person, enjoying a high degree of personal accomplishment, and a treasury of other positive feelings and experiences. You are taking advantage of the chance of a lifetime. Music is the language of the world.

Most importantly, you have chosen to be a part of an organization which has been a proving ground for many of today's most successful people. Your achievements and accomplishments in band are guiding you towards excellence in every part of your life.

We welcome you to Essential Elements Book 2 with the well wishes for continued success on your musical journey. *Strike Up The Band!*

ISBN 0-7935-1283-2

HAL•LEONARD®
CORPORATION
7777 W. BLUEMOUND RD. P.O. BOX 13819 MILWAUKEE, WI 53213

00863534

Sticking Methods

Several methods of sticking are used when playing the snare drum. These include Alternate Sticking (R L R L), Single Hand Sticking (R R R R or L L L L), Right Hand Lead (R on strong divisions of the beat), and Rudimental Sticking (uses basic rudiments). You will see several sticking methods indicated throughout this book. Right Hand Lead exercises are labeled with a ✱, Alternate Sticking exercises are labeled with A, and wrist-builder exercises using Single Hand Sticking are labeled WB. Rudimental exercises show the name of the rudiment the first time it appears above the sticking like this:

When no sticking is indicated, follow your director's instructions on which sticking method to use.

1. HARMONIZED CONCERT B♭ SCALE   Listen to the harmony played by the band.

2. THE ASH GROVE

Old Welsh Air

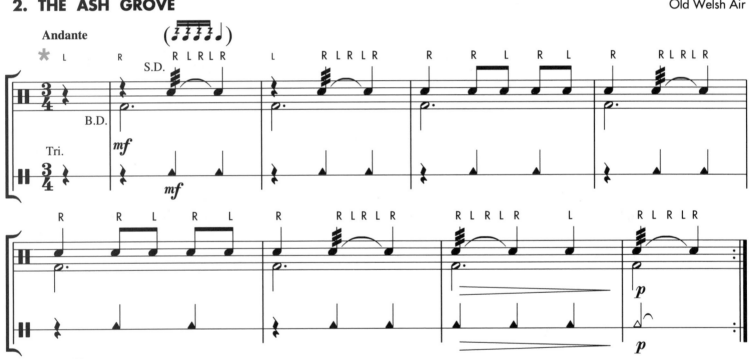

Snares Off

Playing with the snares off produces a hollow tom-tom sound on the snare drum. Another time to turn the snares off is when the drums are NOT playing. This prevents the snares from vibrating and making rattling sounds while the rest of the band is playing. This is especially helpful when the band is playing very softly.

3. METER MANIA   Count carefully!

4. SONG OF KITES

Japanese Children's Song

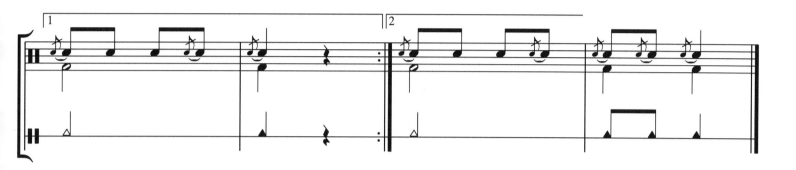

Accidentals   Sharps (♯), flats (♭), or naturals (♮) found in the music but not in the key signature. It is very important that you watch for accidentals when you are playing keyboard percussion instruments.

Double Bounce   A double bounce is a controlled multiple bounce consisting of only two bounces per stroke. Rolls that use double bounces are called open rolls. Begin practicing the following exercise at slow tempos gradually increasing speed to develop smooth double bounce rolls.

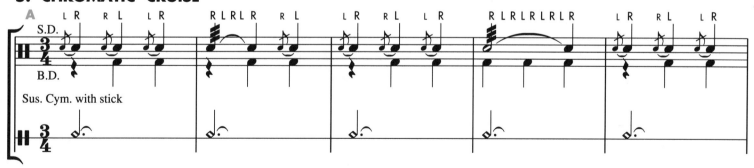

5. CHROMATIC CRUISE

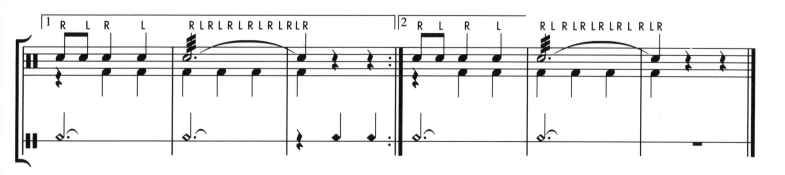

6. TECHNIQUE TRAX

Practice slowly at first, then gradually increase your tempo.
Use the indicated sticking to help build strength in both wrists.

Allegro

Guiro The guiro (pronounced *we' ro*) is a Latin American instrument usually in the shape of a gourd with hollowed-out notches on the side. It is played by scraping a stick along the notched side. A good sound will result if you keep constant pressure on the stick while scraping.

7. SALSA SIESTA - Duet

Play all dynamics carefully.

Moderato

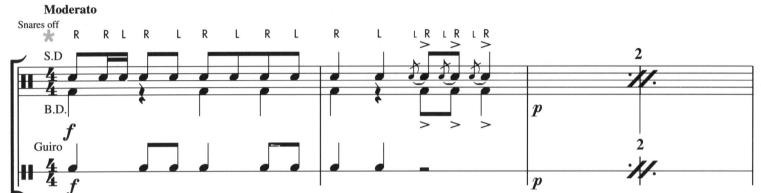

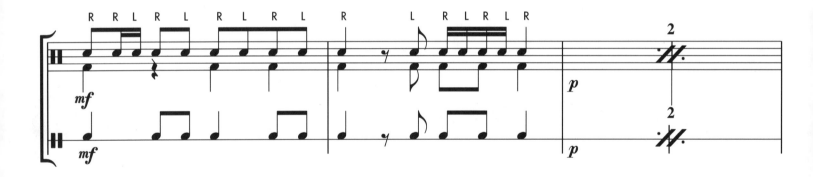

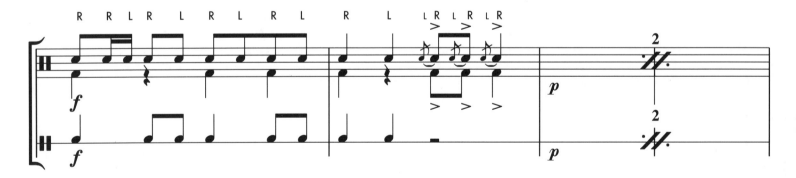

8. RHYTHM ON THE RANGE   Count and clap before playing.

Sightreading Playing a musical selection for the first time. The key to sightreading success is to know what to look for before playing the piece. Follow the guidelines below, and your band will be sightreading STARS! Use the word **STARS** to remind yourself what to look for before reading a selection the first time.

S — **Sharps or flats** in the **key signature**   Identify the key signature first. Silently practice notes from the key signature. Look for key signature changes in the piece.

T — **Time signature** and **tempo markings**   Identify and look for changes in the piece.

A — **Accidentals**   Check for any accidentals not found in the key signature.

R — **Rhythm**   Slowly count and clap all difficult rhythms. Pay special attention to rests.

S — **Signs**   Look for all signs that indicate dynamics, articulations, tempo changes, repeats, 1st and 2nd endings, and any other instructions printed on your music.

Percussionists should check the music carefully to make sure all instruments and mallets are ready before beginning to play.

9. SIGHTREADING CHALLENGE #1

Balance   The proper adjustment of volume and sound from all the instruments in the band playing together. Good balance is achieved when each section of the band can be heard equally. Percussionists should listen carefully to make sure you can always hear the band parts while you play. While playing *Balance Builder* listen carefully and follow your director's instructions to make sure your sound blends with the rest of the band.

Flamadiddle      A snare drum rudiment.

10. BALANCE BUILDER - Chorale

Adagio ◄ Slow tempo, slower than *Andante*.

English composer **Thomas Tallis** (1505-1585) served as a royal court composer during the reigns of Henry VIII, Edward VI, Mary and Elizabeth. The great artist, Michaelangelo, painted the Sistine Chapel during Tallis' lifetime. Canons and rounds were among the popular types of 16th century forms of music that Tallis wrote. Divide into groups and play *Tallis Canon* as a four-part round.

11. TALLIS CANON - Round

Thomas Tallis

Staccato ♩ or 🔸   Staccato notes are marked with a dot above or below the note. Play these notes lightly and with separation. Producing staccato on percussion is different on each instrument. On the snare drum the sound is already separated because of the nature of the instrument, while the bass drum or triangle must be muffled (choked) immediately to produce a staccato effect.

Try the next exercise using any percussion instrument. Experiment with different methods to produce the most staccato sound possible on that instrument.

12. STACCATO STEAMBOAT

13. PAT - A - PAN

Bernard de la Monnoye

Tenuto ♩ or 🔸   Tenuto notes are marked with a straight line above or below the note. Play these notes smooth and connected, holding each note for its full value.

14. TENUTO TIME   Play smooth rolls while the band plays tenutos.

Bass Drum Roll When rolling on the bass drum, use two bass drum mallets of equal size and roll on the same side of the drum, playing on opposite ends of the bass drum head for best resonance.

Ritardando *(ritard.) (rit.)* Gradually slow the tempo.

15. GLOW WORM

Paul Lincke

Allegretto ◄ A lively tempo, faster than *Andante*, but slower than *Allegro*.

*Many famous folk songs are about geographical places. The Scottish folk song *Loch Lomond* is one such folk song. Loch (Lake) Lomond is a lake of Scotland renowned for its breathtaking beauty. Located in the southern highlands, it is almost entirely surrounded by hills. One of these is Ben Lomond, a peak 3,192 feet high.*

16. LOCH LOMOND

Scottish Folk Song

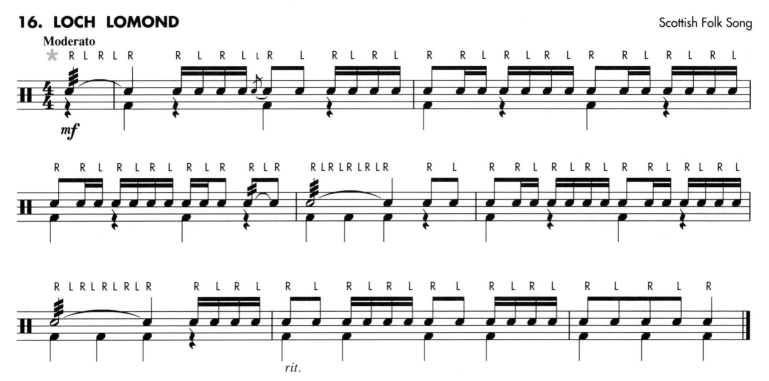

 **Key Change** Sometimes a key signature will change in the middle of a piece of music. You will usually see a thin double bar line at a key change. When you see this thin double bar line in a percussion part, listen closely to the band to see if you can hear the change in key.

Double Paradiddle

A snare drum rudiment.

17. A CHANGE OF KEY   Find all Double Paradiddles in this exercise.

18. CONTRASTS IN B♭ CONCERT

19. ESSENTIAL ELEMENTS QUIZ   Name all rudiments used in this exercise.

Time Signature
(Meter) **Cut Time (Alla Breve)**

¢ or **2/2** - 2 beats per measure
- ♩ or ▬ gets one beat

𝅝	= 2 beats
♩	= 1 beat
♪	= 1/2 beat
♫	= 1/4 beat

Special Percussion Exercise

20. RHYTHM RAP   Count aloud while clapping and tapping.

21. A CUT ABOVE

22. TWO - FOUR DOODLE

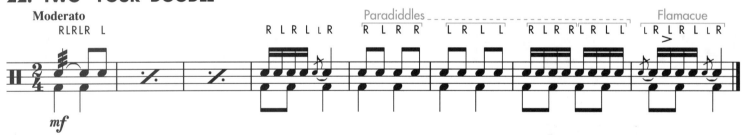

Rolls in Cut Time When playing in cut time, the hand motion for the roll is the same as the counts.
For example:

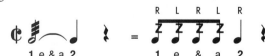

23. CUT - TIME DOODLE

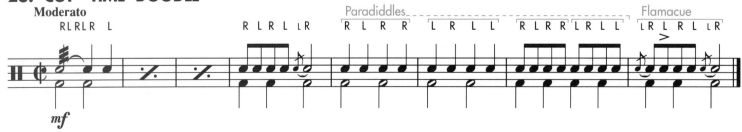

24. MARIANNE

Jamaican Folk Song

25. THE VICTORS MARCH

26. GOOD KING WENCESLAS

27. RHYTHM RAP

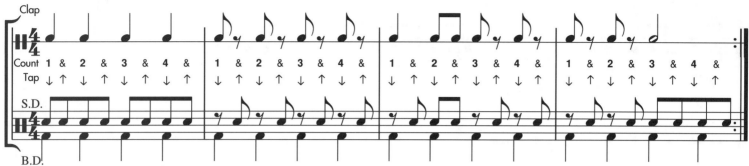

28. EIGHTH NOTES ON THE BEAT

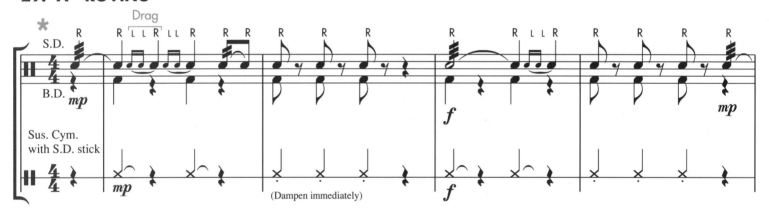

Drag A snare drum rudiment consisting of a double bounce and a single stroke.

Mezzo Piano *mp* Play moderately soft.

29. A - ROVING

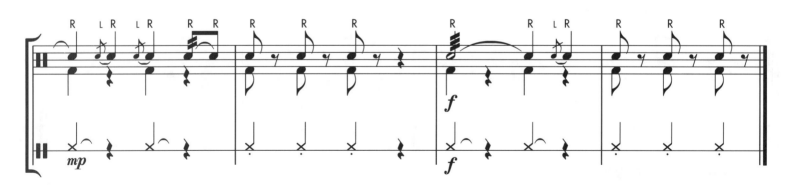

Added Strokes The method in which the snare drum produces notes which sound longer is through the use of adding additional notes to the primary stroke. Listen to the length of the note change as you play the following exercise on snare drum.

30. RHYTHM RAP

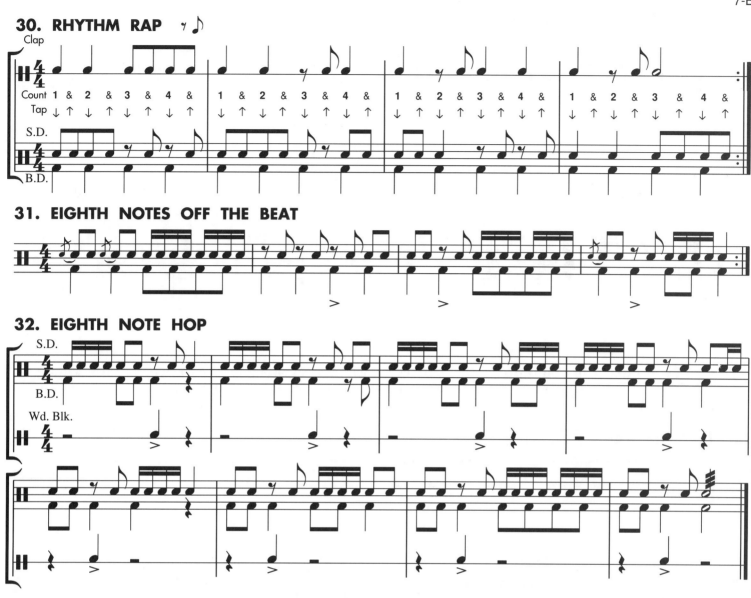

31. EIGHTH NOTES OFF THE BEAT

32. EIGHTH NOTE HOP

Review the **STARS** guidelines before sightreading.

S — Sharps or flats in the key signature
T — Time signature and tempos
A — Accidentals
R — Rhythm
S — Signs

Percussionists should check the music carefully to make sure all instruments and mallets are ready before beginning to play.

33. SIGHTREADING CHALLENGE #2

Where is beat 4?▲

34. CONCERT C SCALE EXERCISE
Play this exercise as a wrist builder, playing the entire exercise with your left hand.

35. THE MINSTREL BOY
Irish Folk Song

Moderato

Theory **Syncopation** In many types of music, the accent or emphasis occurs on notes that do not normally receive a strong pulse or beat. This is called **syncopation** and is very common in jazz, rock and pop, as well as in classical music.

36. RHYTHM RAP

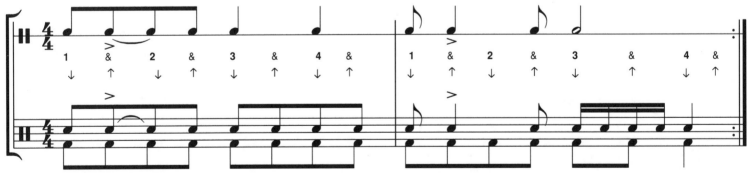

37. SYNCOPATION TIME

38. JODIE'S MARCH

American composer **George M. Cohan** (1878-1942) was also a popular author, producer, director and performer. He helped develop a popular form of American musical theater now known as musical comedy. He is also considered to be one of the most famous composers of American patriotic songs, earning the Congressional Medal of Honor for his works. Many of his songs became morale boosters when the United States entered World War I in 1917.

39. ESSENTIAL ELEMENTS QUIZ - YOU'RE A GRAND OLD FLAG

George M. Cohan

40. RHYTHM RAP

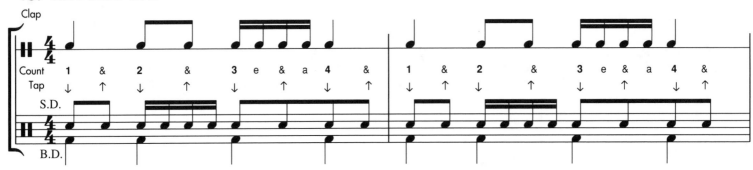

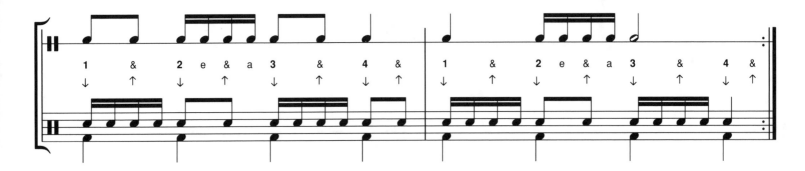

41. SIXTEENTH NOTE FANFARE

42. MOVING ALONG   Practice slowly at first, then gradually increase the tempo.

43. BACK AND FORTH - Duet

Timpani Timpani parts are written in bass clef 𝄢 because the instruments are **tuned** percussion instruments. Each timpani plays one note. To tune each timpani drum, identify the tuning notes from your music. Use an electronic tuner or keyboard percussion instrument, and play one tuning note. Lightly tap your fingers on the head of one drum and compare with the tuning note pitch. Slowly adjust the tuning pedal to match the written note. Repeat for each timpani. Ask your director for assistance. Use medium hard timpani mallets, unless directed otherwise. Timp. is the abbreviation for timpani.

44. SHE'LL BE COMIN' 'ROUND THE MOUNTAIN - Variation

45. SIGHTREADING CHALLENGE #3   Review the STARS guidelines before sightreading.

Moderato   Find all Flamacues and Paradiddles in this exercise.

Rallentando *(rall.)* Gradually slow the tempo. (Same as *ritardando*.)

46. WARM - UP CHORALE - Duet

Begin rolls with the right hand and play all ♪'s with the right hand. Next time start with the left hand. Also play this exercise with alternating hands to develop even sounds. Work for smooth rolls.

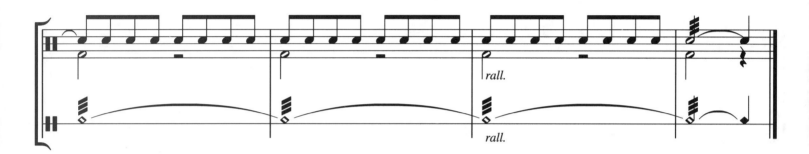

47. IRISH JIG

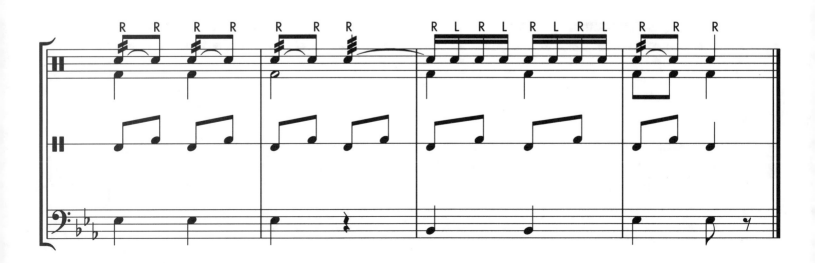

English composer **Sir Edward Elgar** (1857-1934) received his musical training from his father. Elgar's most famous piece, *Pomp and Circumstance,* was written for the coronation of King Edward VII in 1901, the same year the United States inaugurated its 26th President, Theodore Roosevelt — the youngest man to ever hold the office.

Legato   Play in a smooth and connected style, as if all notes were marked with *tenutos*.

48. POMP AND CIRCUMSTANCE - Duet

Sir Edward Elgar

49. TECHNIQUE TRAX

50. ESSENTIAL ELEMENTS QUIZ   Both snare drum parts should be played by one player.

56. CONCERT A♭ REVIEW   Strive for smooth and even rolls.

57. BILL BAILEY   The suspended cymbal and snare drum should be played by one player using right hand on the cymbal and left hand on the snare drum.   Hughie Cannon

Allegro

58. RHYTHM RAP

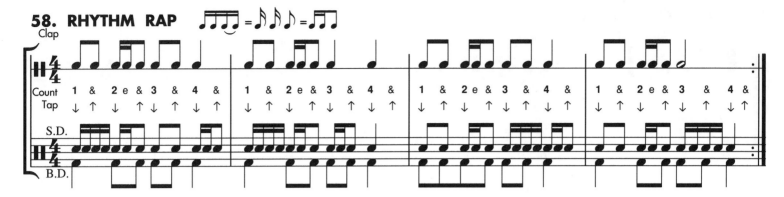

Etude A "study piece" designed to teach a specific musical technique.

59. RHYTHM ETUDE

Both snare drum parts should be played by one player, using the right hand on the rim and the left hand on the head.

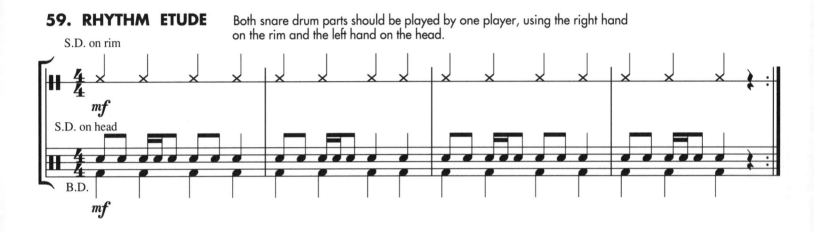

Triangle Roll Roll between the lower closed corner of the triangle using rapid stick motion between the bottom and the side.

60. ENGLISH DANCE

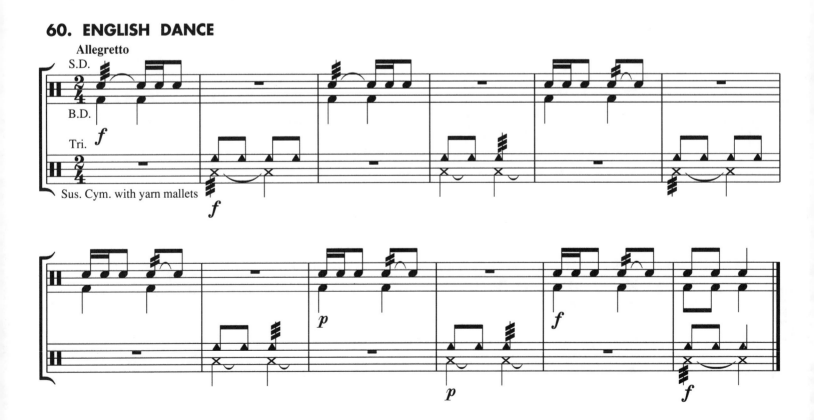

61. THE THUNDERER

John Philip Sousa

62. CHANGING OF THE GUARD

Keep crescendos even. Be careful not to get loud too quickly.

Review the **STARS** guidelines before sightreading.

S — Sharps or flats in the key signature
T — Time signature and tempos
A — Accidentals
R — Rhythm
S — Signs

Percussionists should check the music carefully to make sure all instruments and mallets are ready before beginning to play.

63. SIGHTREADING CHALLENGE #4

64. RHYTHM RAP

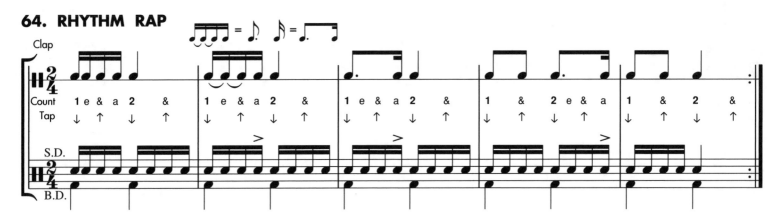

Timpani Roll ♪ Rapidly alternate single strokes as smoothly as possible. Release on the tied note or final beat. The hand that starts the roll releases it.

65. MARCHING ALONG

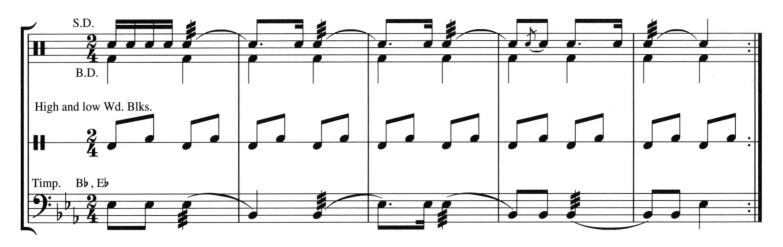

66. FANFARE FOR BAND - Trio   Listen to the band's harmony.

Maestoso ◄ Play in a majestic, stately manner.

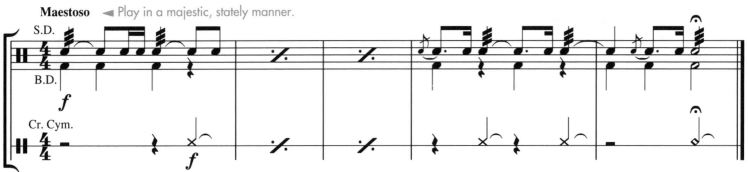

67. ARIA FROM THE MARRIAGE OF FIGARO

Wolfgang Amadeus Mozart

History

French composer **Georges Bizet** (1838-1875) entered the Paris Conservatory to study music when he was only ten years old. There he won many awards for voice, piano, organ, and composition. Bizet is best known for his opera *Carmen*, which was first performed in 1875. *Carmen* showed the new interest of the nineteenth century in the common people; it was about Gypsies and soldiers, smugglers and outlaws. At first people were shocked to see such realism on stage, but *Carmen* was soon hailed as the most popular French opera ever written.

68. ESSENTIAL ELEMENTS QUIZ - TOREADOR MARCH FROM CARMEN

Georges Bizet

69. TANGO - (LA CUMPARSITA)

Spanish Folk Dance

70. THE YELLOW ROSE OF TEXAS

Listen to how the character of this piece changes in the second half when the rudiments are added.

Flamacue

71. CONCERT E♭ SCALE AND ARPEGGIO

Play as a wrist builder using the indicated sticking.

72. ETUDE IN THIRDS   Use paradiddle sticking throughout.

American composer **John Philip Sousa** (1854-1932) was best known for his brilliant band marches. Although he wrote 136 marches, *The Stars and Stripes Forever* became one of his most famous and was declared the official march of the United States of America in 1987.

73. THE STARS AND STRIPES FOREVER

John Philip Sousa

Time Signature
(Meter)

6 - 6 beats per measure
8 - ♪ or 𝄾 gets one beat

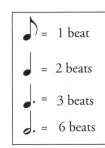

There are two ways to count **6/8** time:

6 beats to a measure with the eighth note receiving 1 beat. OR 2 beats to a measure with 3 eighth notes (or its equivalent) receiving one beat.

Slower music is usually counted in 6, while faster music is counted in 2. Start by counting 6 beats to a measure, placing a slight accent on beats 1 and 4 when tapping and counting aloud.

74. RHYTHM RAP

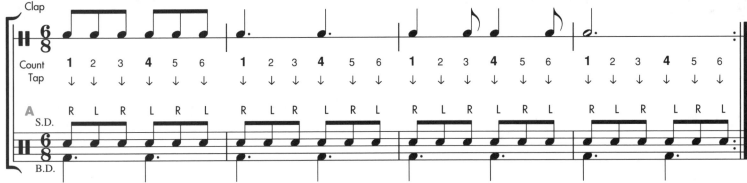

Flam Accents — A snare drum rudiment

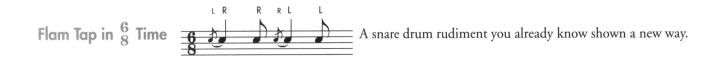

Flam Tap in 6/8 Time — A snare drum rudiment you already know shown a new way.

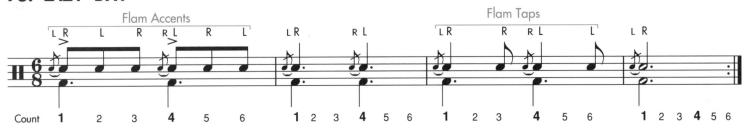

75. LAZY DAY

76. FRENCH FOLK TUNE

Multiple Bounce In ⁶⁄₈ Time ♪♪♪ Use the sticking pattern from the eighth note pulse and connect with multiple bounces to sound as smooth as possible.

77. ROW YOUR BOAT
The first time through, count and play slowly in 6.
Then try playing faster, tapping 2 beats per measure.

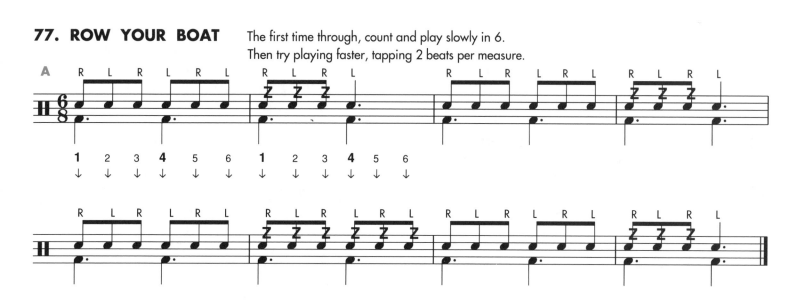

78. JOLLY GOOD FELLOW

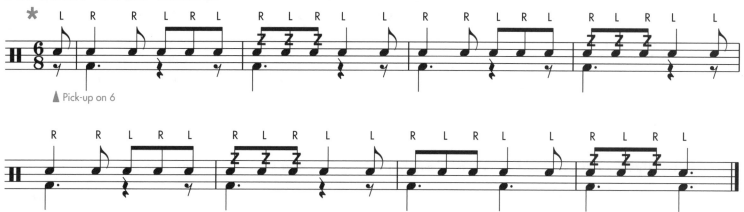

▲ Pick-up on 6

79. ESSENTIAL ELEMENTS QUIZ - WHEN JOHNNY COMES MARCHING HOME

Allegro

mf

Where is beat 6? ▲

Theory **Enharmonics** Notes that have different letter names but share the same bar on the keyboard percussion instruments. When playing keyboard percussion, it is very helpful to be familiar with enharmonic notes.

Theory **Chromatic Scale** A scale made up of consecutive half-steps. (A half-step is the smallest distance between 2 notes.) Usually chromatic scales are written with sharps (♯) going up and flats (♭) going down. The following exercise shows a chromatic scale which you may play on any keyboard percussion instrument.

80. CHROMATIC SCALE WARM - UP   Play as a snare drum wrist builder using the indicated sticking.

81. TECHNIQUE TRAX   The top two lines should be played by one player to develop independence of hands.

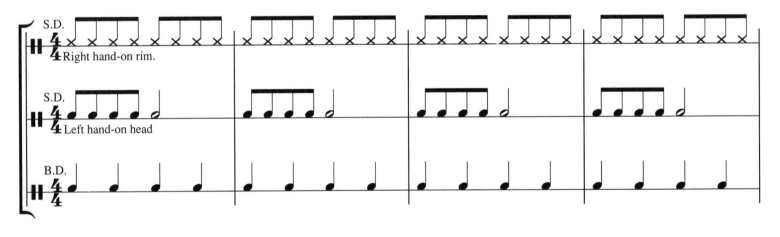

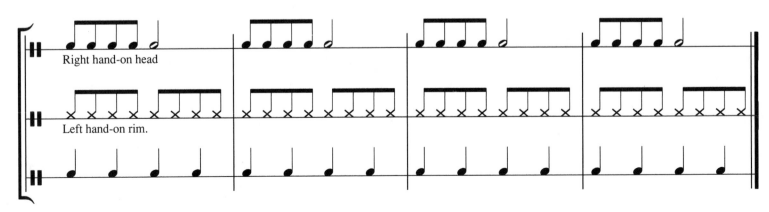

A **Habañera** is a dance in slow $\frac{2}{4}$ meter. It is named after the capital of Cuba, although it was made most popular in Spain during the 1800's by flamenco dancers. One of the most famous Habañeras is heard in Bizet's *Carmen*, written in 1875.

82. HABAÑERA

Georges Bizet

83. CHROMATIC CRESCENDO

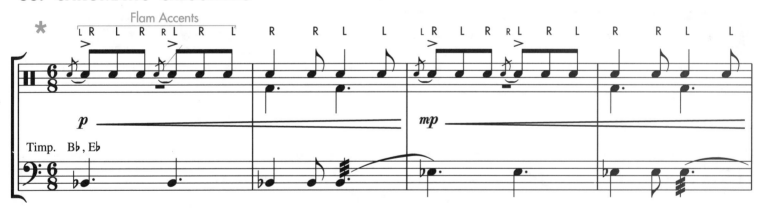

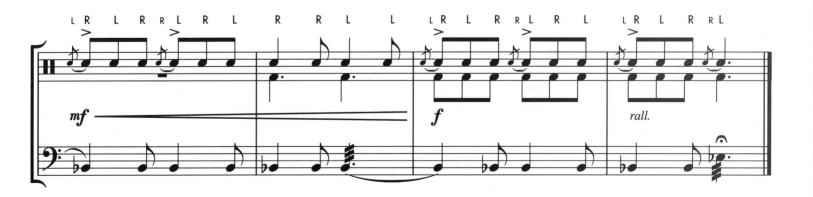

84. TURKISH MARCH

Ludwig van Beethoven

85. THE OVERLANDER

Australian Folk Song

86. STACCATO TIME

Allegro

87. YANKEE DOODLE DANDY

George M. Cohan

Review the **STARS** guidelines before sightreading.

S — Sharps or flats in the key signature
T — Time signature and tempos
A — Accidentals
R — Rhythm
S — Signs

Percussionists should check the music carefully to make sure all instruments and mallets are ready before beginning to play.

88. SIGHTREADING CHALLENGE #5

Listen for the key change.

Triplets A triplet is a group of three notes. In $\frac{2}{4}$, $\frac{3}{4}$, or $\frac{4}{4}$ time, an eighth note triplet is played in one beat.

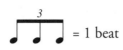 = 1 beat

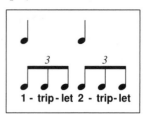

89. RHYTHM RAP

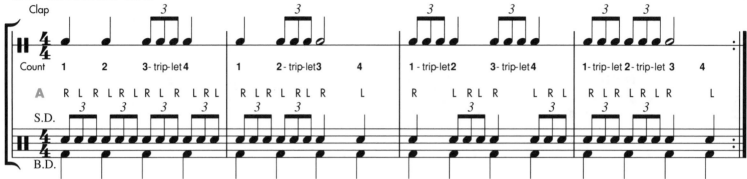

90. THREE TO GET READY

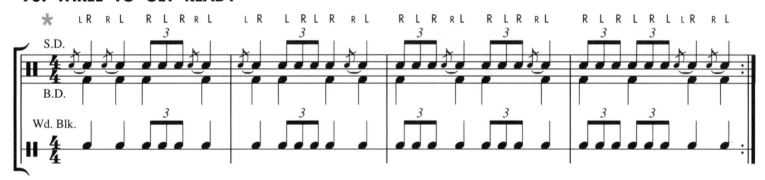

91. CONCERT E♭ SCALE WITH TRIPLETS

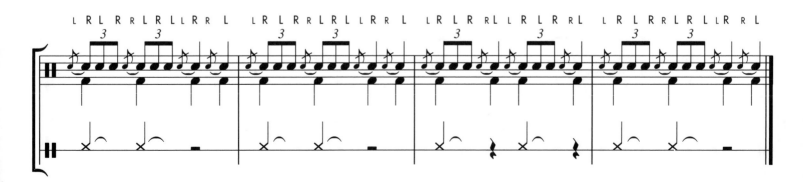

92. MARCH FROM THE NUTCRACKER - Duet

Peter I. Tchaikovsky

93. THEME FROM FAUST

Charles Gounod

94. CONCERT F SCALE
Play as a wrist builder using the indicated sticking.

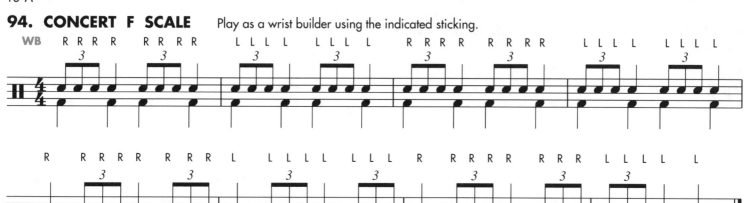

95. ETUDE IN THIRDS
The top two lines should be played by one player to develop independence of hands.

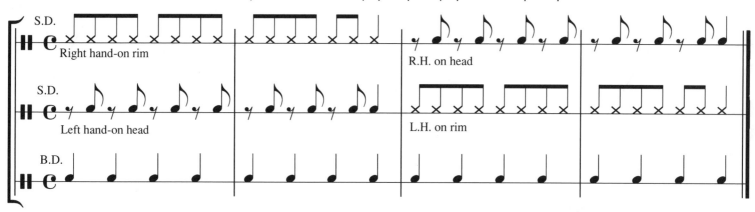

96. RHYTHM RAP

97. ON THE MOVE

98. CLIMBING HIGHER

99. ARKANSAS TRAVELER

100. ESSENTIAL ELEMENTS QUIZ

History The Marines' Hymn was written in 1847 during the Mexican War by a Marine Corps poet who set the original lyrics to music from an old French opera. Some of the words refer to the Mexican War. The Treaty of Guadalupe Hidalgo (1848) ended the war. By its terms, Mexico recognized the U.S.'s annexation of Texas and California.

101. THE MARINES' HYMN

102. TECHNIQUE TRAX   Practice slowly at first, then gradually increase the tempo to *Allegro*.

D.S. al Fine Play until you see the *D.S. al Fine*, then go back to the sign (𝄋) and play until you see the word *Fine* (finish). D.S. is the Latin abbreviation for *Dal segno*, "from the sign."

103. D.S. MARCH

Accelerando *(accel.)* Gradually increase the tempo.

104. CAN - CAN

Jacques Offenbach

▲Follow your director's accelerating tempo.

105. $\frac{6}{8}$ STUDY WITH ARPEGGIO

Play as a wrist builder using the indicated sticking.

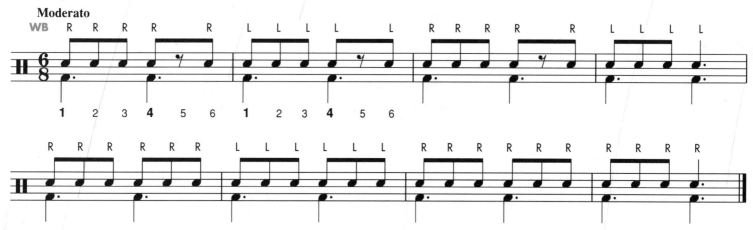

The **waltz** is a dance in moderate $\frac{3}{4}$ time which developed about 1800 from the Ländler, an Austrian peasant dance. When the waltz was first introduced to the dance floor, it was very controversial because this was the first time partners danced in an embracing position. Austrian composer **Johann Strauss** (1825-1899) composed over 400 waltzes. These include such famous pieces as *The Blue Danube, Tales From the Vienna Woods* and *Emperor Waltz*.

106. EMPORER WALTZ

Johann Strauss

107. ENGLISH DANCE - Duet   Listen to the band's harmony.   J.C. Bach

108. ESSENTIAL ELEMENTS QUIZ - BRITISH GRENADIERS

109. TECHNIQUE TRAX Play as a wrist builder using the indicated sticking.

110. UNFINISHED SYMPHONY THEME Franz Schubert

111. RHYTHM TRICKS Count and clap before playing.

112. COUNTRY GARDENS

English Folk Song

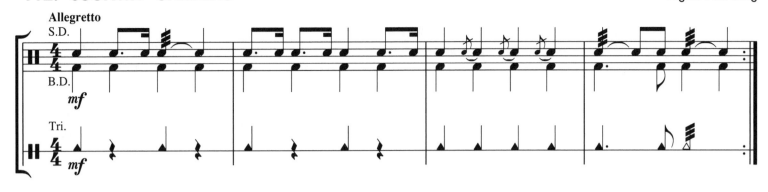

113. JOSHUA

Black American Spiritual

114. LISTEN TO THE MOCKINGBIRD

Alice Hawthorne

Moderato

mf

Russian composer **Reinhold Gliére** (1875-1956) based his melodies on folk music of the Russian people. Having music reflect the culture of the composer's country was a trend which appeared in much art and music during the late 19th and early 20th centuries. *Russian Sailors' Dance* is an example of such musical Nationalism. It is from his ballet *The Red Poppy*, written in 1927.

115. RUSSIAN SAILORS' DANCE

Reinhold Gliére

Allegro
S.D.

B.D.

f

Continue playing in the same style.

Fine   R L R L R   R L R L R   *simile*

mf

Go back to the beginning.

D.C. al Fine

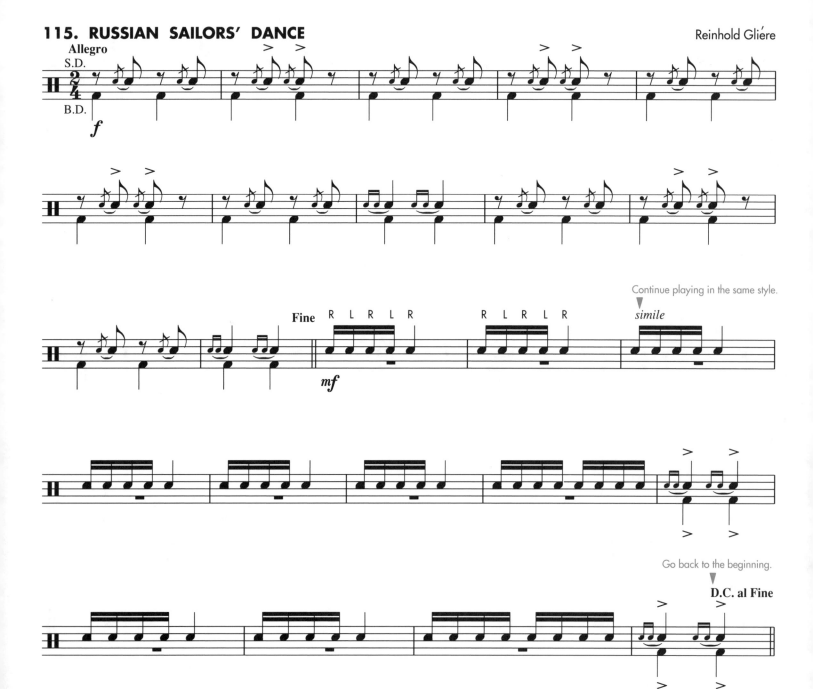

116. ANCHORS AWEIGH

Capt. Alfred H. Miles
and Charles A. Zimmerman

117. FUNERAL MARCH OF A MARIONETTE

Charles Gounod

D.S. al Coda Play until you see *D.S. al Coda*, then go back to the sign (𝄋) and play until you see the words "*To Coda.*" Skip to the *coda* and play until the end. D.S. is the Latin abbreviation for *dal segno*, "from the sign." *Coda* means "tail" or conclusion.

118. SIMPLE GIFTS - Full Band Arrangement

Shaker Folk Song
Arr. by John Higgins

119. DANNY BOY - Full Band Arrangement

Arr. by John Higgins

Snare Drum, Bass Drum

119. DANNY BOY - Full Band Arrangement

Arr. by John Higgins

Triangle, Sus. Cym.

120. SEMPER FIDELIS - Full Band Arrangement

John Philip Sousa
Arr. by John Higgins

Snare Drum, Bass Drum

121. TAKE ME OUT TO THE BALLGAME - Full Band Arrangement

Arr. by John Higgins

Snare Drum, Bass Drum

121. TAKE ME OUT TO THE BALLGAME - Full Band Arrangement

Arr. by John Higgins

Wood Block, Triangle, Cr. Cym.

122. SERENGETI (AN AFRICAN RHAPSODY)

By John Higgins

Bass Drum, Tom-Toms, Guiro, Bongos

122. SERENGETI (AN AFRICAN RHAPSODY)

By John Higgins

Theory **Major Scale** A **Major Scale** is a series of eight notes that follow a definite pattern of whole steps and half steps. Half steps appear only between scale steps 3-4 and 7-8. Every major scale has the same arrangement of whole steps and half steps.

The following exercise shows one of the band's most common major scales. Listen as the band plays or play along on any keyboard percussion instrument.

123. CONCERT B♭ MAJOR SCALE

Exercises 124-129 allow the band to learn several different major scales. Your director may want you to play major scales also using the keyboard percussion book. Otherwise you may play along on snare drum using the following sticking exercises.

124. CONCERT E♭ MAJOR SCALE   (Paradiddles & L.H. Double Paradiddles)

125. CONCERT F MAJOR SCALE   (Paradiddles & R.H. Double Paradiddles)

126. CONCERT A♭ MAJOR SCALE   (Flamadiddles & L.H. Double Flamadiddles)

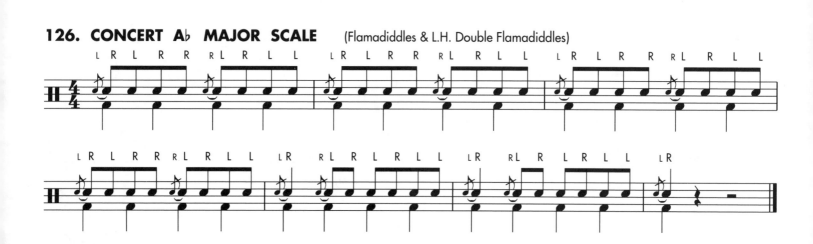

127. CONCERT C MAJOR SCALE (Flamadiddles & R.H. Double Flamadiddles)

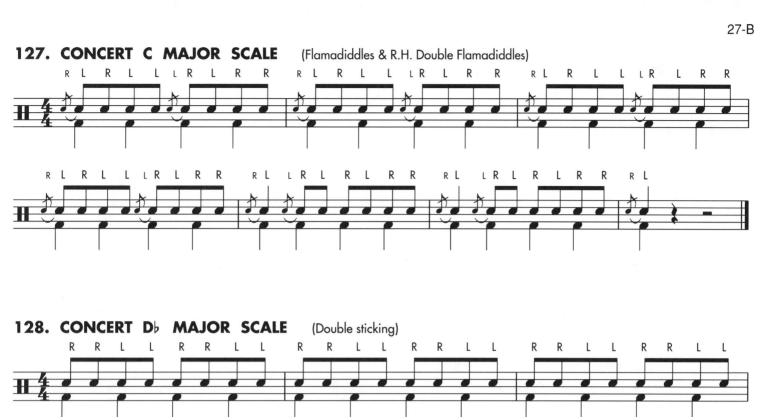

128. CONCERT D♭ MAJOR SCALE (Double sticking)

129. CONCERT G MAJOR SCALE ("Tricky" Double sticking)

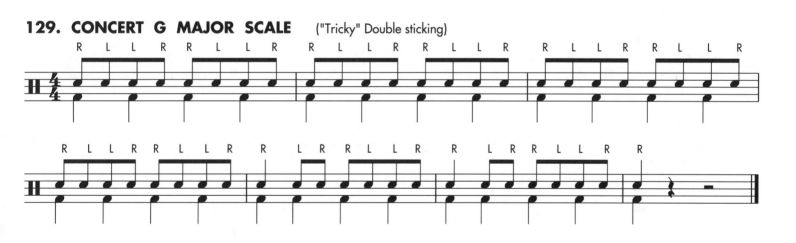

130. SPECIAL KEYBOARD PERCUSSION CHROMATIC SCALE

1st time: R L R L
2nd time: L R L R

SPECIAL PERCUSSION EXERCISES

ROLL REVIEW EXERCISES

The following roll exercises will help you become more familiar with the basic hand motion required to play smooth sounding rolls. Each roll exercise is divided into two parts. (You will see a thin double bar line dividing the two parts.) Playing the first part of each exercise with the correct hand motion will prepare you for the correct playing of the rolls in the second part of the exercise. Remember: Your hand motion should be the same in both parts of the exercise. The only difference is that you add multiple or double bounces to the sixteenth note hand motion when you play the rolls.

Rolls in Cut Time When playing rolls in cut time, add multiple or double bounces to the eighth note hand motion.

ADDITIONAL STUDIES IN $\frac{6}{8}$ METER

It is very important for percussionists to be familiar with sixteenth notes in $\frac{6}{8}$ meter since this is the rhythmic pulse for playing rolls in $\frac{6}{8}$. Play the following exercises slowly at first, then gradually increase your tempo. Use alternate sticking patterns unless your director tells you otherwise.

Rolls In $\frac{6}{8}$ Meter When playing rolls in $\frac{6}{8}$, the best sound can be achieved by adding multiple or double bounces to the sixteenth note hand motion.

EXERCISES IN PLAYING ACCENTS

Playing accents in the correct places in your music not only makes your part more interesting, but also helps the rest of the band play their parts better. Pay very close attention to the accents while playing the next exercises. Start these exercises slowly at first, then gradually increase your tempo.

A. ACCENT CHALLENGE #1

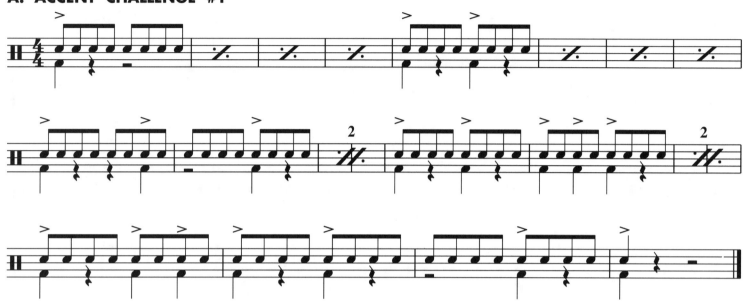

B. ACCENT CHALLENGE #2

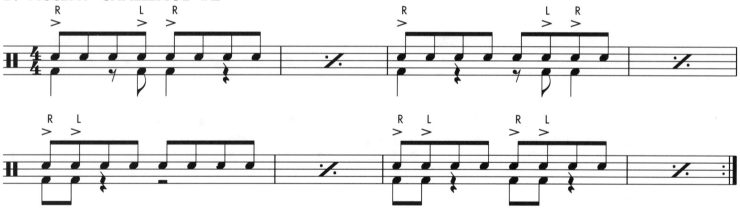

C. ACCENT CHALLENGE #3

EXERCISES IN INDEPENDENCE

The following exercises will help you to develop the ability to play more than one line of music at the same time. This is a very valuable skill for all percussionists to learn. On the next three exercises, the top line of music should be played with your right hand, while the bottom line should be played with your left hand. Use two drums with different pitches or use one drum with one hand playing on the head of the drum and the other hand playing on the rim.

A. INDEPENDENCE WORK - OUT #1

B. INDEPENDENCE WORK - OUT #2

C. INDEPENDENCE WORK - OUT #3

D. INDEPENDENCE WORK - OUT #4

BASIC PERCUSSION EXERCISES

DYNAMIC STICKING CONTROL

Practice these exercises during your daily warm-up. Begin with slow tempos and gradually increase your speed. Play crescendos and decrescendos smoothly and evenly.

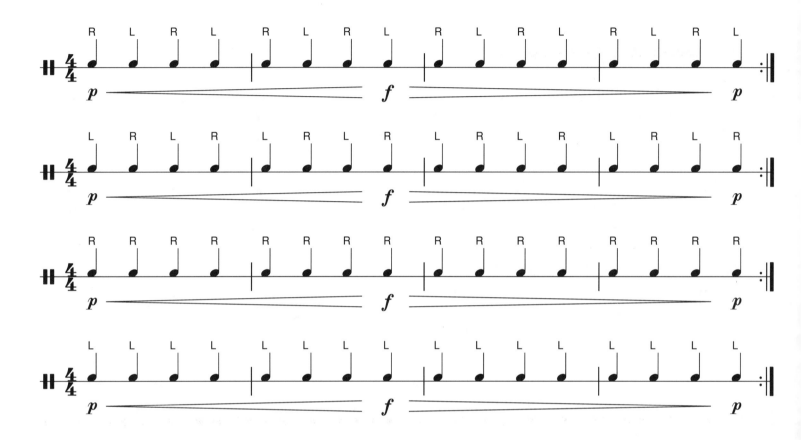

ROLLS WITHOUT RELEASE NOTES

You will often find rolls that are not connected to a release note. When you see this, simply roll for the full value of the note and lift both hands off the drum at the end of the count:

When non-release rolls follow each other, put a very slight separation between them. Lift the sticks and start the next roll on time:

Percussionists must always listen and make their parts "fit" what is happening in the band at the same time. Play smooth and connected rolls when the band plays *legato*. Separate rolls during *marcato*, or accented sections. When in doubt, ask your conductor.

SNARE DRUM INTERNATIONAL DRUM RUDIMENTS

All rudiments should be practiced: open (slow) to close (fast) and/or at an even moderate march tempo.

Take Special Care
Snare drums occasionally need tuning. Ask your teacher to help you tighten each tension rod equally using a drum key.
• Be careful not to over-tighten the head. It will break if the tension is too tight.
• Loosen the snare strainer at the end of each rehearsal.
• Cover all percussion instruments when not in use.
• Put sticks away in a storage area. Keep the percussion section neat!
• Sticks are the only things which should be placed on the snare drum. NEVER put or allow others to put objects on any percussion instrument.

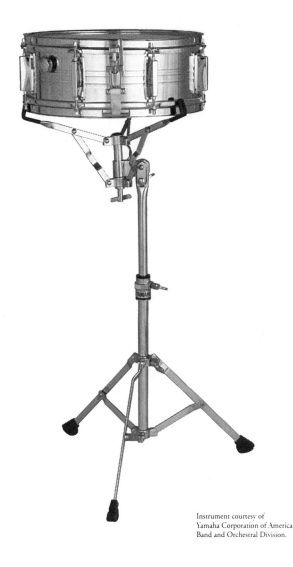

Instrument courtesy of Yamaha Corporation of America Band and Orchestral Division.

I. ROLL RUDIMENTS

A. SINGLE STROKE ROLL RUDIMENTS

1. Single Stroke Roll

3. Single Stroke Seven

2. Single Stroke Four

B. MULTIPLE BOUNCE ROLL RUDIMENTS

4. Multiple Bounce Roll

R R R R R R R R L L L L L L L L

5. Triple Stroke Roll

R R R L L L R R R L L L

C. DOUBLE STROKE OPEN ROLL RUDIMENTS

6. Double Stroke Open Roll

R R L L R R L L

7. Five Stroke Roll

R   R   L   L

8. Six Stroke Roll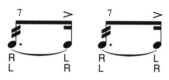

R   L   R   L
L   R   L   R

9. Seven Stroke Roll

R   L   R   L
L   R   L   R

10. Nine Stroke Roll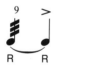

R   R   L   L

11. Ten Stroke Roll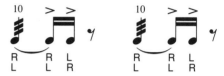

R   R L   R   R L
L   L R   L   L R

12. Eleven Stroke Roll

R   R L   R   R L
L   L R   L   L R

13. Thirteen Stroke Roll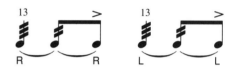

R   R   L   L

14. Fifteen Stroke Roll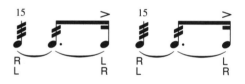

R   L   R   L
L   R   L   R

15. Seventeen Stroke Roll

R   R   L   L

II. DIDDLE RUDIMENTS

16. Single Paradiddle

R L R R   L R L L

17. Double Paradiddle

R L R L R R   L R L R L L

18. Triple Paradiddle

R L R L R L R R   L R L R L R L L

19. Single Paradiddle-Diddle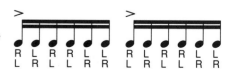

R L R R L L   R L R R L L
L R L L R R   L R L L R R

III. FLAM RUDIMENTS

20. Flam

21. Flam Accent

22. Flam Tap

23. Flamacue

24. Flam Paradiddle

25. Single Flammed Mill

26. Flam Paradiddle-Diddle

27. Pataflafla
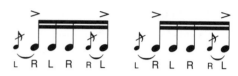

28. Swiss Army Triplet

29. Inverted Flam Tap

30. Flam Drag

IV. DRAG RUDIMENTS

31. Drag

32. Single Drag Tap

33. Double Drag Tap

34. Lesson 25

35. Single Dragadiddle

36. Drag Paradiddle #1

37. Drag Paradiddle #2

38. Single Ratamacue

39. Double Ratamacue

40. Triple Ratamacue

KEYBOARD PERCUSSION INSTRUMENTS

Each keyboard percussion instrument has a unique sound because of the materials used to create the instrument. Ranges may differ with some models of instruments.

Take Special Care
- Cover all percussion instruments when they are not being used.
- Put mallets away in a storage area. Keep the percussion section neat!
- Mallets are the only things which should be placed on your instrument. NEVER put or allow others to put objects on any percussion instrument.

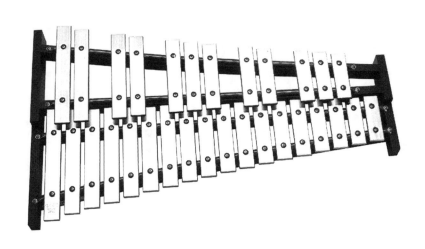

BELLS (Orchestra Bells)
- Bars - metal alloy or steel
- Mallets - lexan (hard plastic), brass or hard rubber
- Range - 2 1/2 octaves
- Sounds 2 octaves higher than written

XYLOPHONE
- Bars - wooden or synthetic
- Mallets- hard rubber
- Range - 3 octaves
- Sounds 1 octave higher than written

MARIMBA

- Bars - wooden (wider than xylophone bars) Resonating tube located below each bar
- Mallets - soft to medium rubber or yarn covered
- Range - 4 1/2 octaves (reads bass and treble clefs)
- Sounding pitch is the same as written pitch

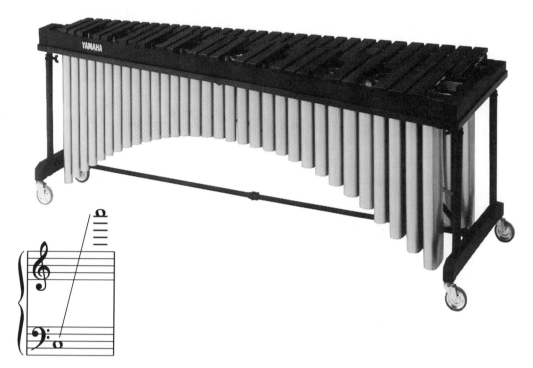

VIBRAPHONE

- Bars - metal alloy or aluminum Resonating tubes located below each bar Adjustable electric fans in each resonator create "vibrato" effect
- Mallets - yarn covered
- Range - 3 octaves
- Sounding pitch is the same as written pitch

CHIMES

- Bars - metal tubes
- Mallets - plastic, rawhide or wooden
- Range - 1 1/2 octaves
- Sounding pitch is the same as written pitch

GLOSSARY

Essential Element	Definition	Essential Element	Definition
Accelerando *accel.*	Gradually increase the tempo.	Legato	Play in a smooth and connected style.
Accent	Emphasize the note.	Leger Lines	Adds notes outside of the music staff.
Accidentals	Sharps, flats, and naturals found in the music.	Maestoso	Play in a majestic, stately manner.
Adagio	Slow tempo, slower than *Andante*.	Major Scale	Series of 8 notes with a definite pattern of whole steps and half steps.
Alla Breve	Another name for cut time.	Measure	A segment of music divided by bar lines.
Allegretto	A lively tempo.		
Allegro	Fast bright tempo.	Measure Repeat	Repeat the previous measure.
Andante	Slow walking tempo.	*mezzo forte* **mf**	Play moderately loud.
Arpeggio	A sequence of notes from any scale.	*mezzo piano* **mp**	Play moderately soft.
Balance	The proper adjustment of volume from all instruments.	Moderato	Moderate tempo.
		Multiple Measures Rest	The number indicates how many measures to count and rest.
Bar Lines	Divide the music staff into measures.		
Bass Clef	"F" clef used by trbs., bar, bsn. and tuba.	Music Staff	Lines and spaces where notes are placed.
Bizet, Georges	French composer (1838-1875).	Natural Sign ♮	Cancels a flat ♭ or sharp ♯ in the measure.
Breath Mark '	Take a deep breath after playing the note full value.		
Chromatics	Notes that are altered with sharps, flats and naturals.	*piano* **p**	Play softly.
		Pick-up Notes	Note or notes that come before the first full measure.
Chromatic Scale	Sequence of notes in half-steps.	Rallentando *rall.*	Gradually slow the tempo.
Cohan, George M.	American composer (1878-1942).	Rehearsal Numbers	Measure numbers in squares above the staff.
Common Time **C**	Another way to write 4/4.		
Crescendo	Gradually increase volume	Repeat Sign	Go back to the beginning and play again.
Cut Time **¢**	Meter in which the half note gets one beat.		Repeat the section of music enclosed by repeat signs.
D.C. al Fine	*Da Capo al Fine* - Play until *D.C. al Fine*. Go back to the beginning and play until *Fine*.	Rests	Silent beats of music.
		Ritardando *rit.*	Gradually slow the tempo.
D.S. al Fine	*Del Segno al Fine* - Play until *D.S. al Fine*. Go back to the sign (𝄋) and play until *Fine*.	Round or Canon	Musical form where instruments play the same melody entering at different times.
Decrescendo	Gradually decrease volume.	Sharp ♯	Raises the note and remains in effect the entire measure.
Dotted Note	The dot adds half the value of the note.		
Double Bar	Indicates the end of a piece of music.	Sightreading	Playing a musical selection for the first time.
Duet	Composition for two players.	Simile *sim.*	Continue in the same style.
Dynamics	The volume of music.	Slur	A curved line that connects notes of different pitches.
Edgar, Sir Edward	English composer (1857-1934).		
Enharmonics	Notes that are written differently but sound the same.	Sousa, John Philip	American composer (1854-1932).
		Staccato	Play the notes with separation.
Etude	A "study piece" for a technique.	Strauss, Johann	Austrian composer (1825-1899).
Fermata ⌢	Hold the note longer, or until your director tells you to release it.	Syncopation	Accents on the weak beats of the music.
1st and 2nd Endings	Play the 1st ending the 1st time through. Then, repeat the same music, skip the 1st ending and play the 2nd.	Tallis, Thomas	English composer (1505-1585).
		Tempo	The speed of music.
		Tenuto	Play notes for their full value.
		Tie	A curved line that connects notes of the same pitch.
Flat ♭	Lowers the note and remains in effect the entire measure.	Time Signature (Meter)	Tells how many beats are in each measure and what kind of note gets one beat.
forte **f**	Play loudly.		
Gliére, Reinhold	Russian composer (1875-1956).		
Habañera	Dance in slow 2/4 meter.	Treble Clef	"G" clef used by fls., ob., clar., sax. and tpt.
Half-step	The smallest distance between two notes.		
Interval	The numerical distance between two notes.	Trio	Composition for three players.
		Triplet	Group of three notes.
Key Signature	Flats or sharps next to the clef that apply to entire piece.	Waltz	Dance in moderate 3/4 meter.